INSECTS

Daniel J. Bickel

INTRODUCTION

Insects are found in many places—in gardens, woods, fields, your house, and sometimes buzzing around your head. Some live in water, while others live on dry land, or even in the soil. These fascinating creatures come in many colors, shapes, and sizes, from tiny mosquitoes to large, spectacular butterflies.

All insects have six legs and three main body parts—head, thorax, and abdomen. But the most remarkable thing is that most of them fly. Wings allow many insects to travel long distances and to escape from enemies.

It is easy to collect and keep most insects—you could raise moths from caterpillars or start an ant farm. Some insects bite or sting and should be handled carefully, but most are harmless.

By using this

□ NATIONAL GEOGRAPHIC
my first pocket Guide

INSECTS

Text: Anne Matthews
Illustrations: Simone End
Consultant: Daniel J. Bickel

Copyright © 1996 by the National Geographic Society

First Trade Edition 2001

Published by
The National Geographic Society
John M. Fahey, Jr., President and Chief Executive Officer
Gilbert M. Grosvenor, Chairman of the Board
Nina D. Hoffman, Executive Vice President,
President of Books and School Publishing
William R. Gray, Vice President and Director, Book Division
Nancy Laties Feresten, Director of Children's Publishing
Barbara Brownell, Director of Continuities
Mark A. Caraluzzi, Vice President, Sales and Marketing
Vincent P. Ryan, Manufacturing Manager

Library of Congress Catalog Number: 96-66279

ISBN: 0-7922-3418-9

Trade Edition ISBN: 0-7922-6570-X

Produced for the National Geographic Society by Weldon Owen Pty Ltd
43 Victoria Street, McMahons Point, NSW 2060, Australia
A member of the Weldon Owen Group of Companies
Sydney • San Francisco • London

Chairman: Kevin Weldon
President: John Owen
Publisher: Sheena Coupe
Managing Editor: Ariana Klepac
Art Director: Sue Burk
Senior Designer: Mark Thacker
Designer: Regina Safro
Text Editors: Robert Coupe, Paulette Kay
Photo Researcher: Elizabeth Connolly
Production Director: Mick Bagnato
Production Manager: Simone Perryman

Film production by Mandarin Offset
Printed in Mexico

book, and a magnifying glass, you will be able to recognize insects that you find, and learn about how they live.

HOW TO USE THIS BOOK

Each spread in this book helps you to identify one kind of insect. There is information about the insect's size, color, appearance, and behavior. If you find an insect, you can see how long it is by measuring it on the ruler that you will find in the inside of the back cover. "Where To Find" has a map of North America that is shaded to show you where the insect lives. It also describes its typical home. You will discover an unusual fact about the insect in the "Field Note," and see it in its natural environment in the photograph. If you find a word you do not know, you can look it up in the Glossary on page 76.

MAYFLY

Adult mayflies lead busy and energetic lives. They live from just a few hours to one or two days. In this short time, the female flits about to find a mate, lays her eggs, then dies.

WHERE TO FIND:
Mayfly larvae (LAR-vee) and nymphs (NIMFS) feed in ponds and streams where female mayflies lay eggs.

WHAT TO LOOK FOR:

✳ **SIZE**
Mayflies are usually between a half inch and one inch long.

✳ **COLOR**
They are a dull greenish-brown color.

✳ **OTHER FEATURES**
They have long soft bodies, large eyes, and small legs.

✳ **BEHAVIOR**
Males sometimes fly in large groups, called swarms. They fly up and down, rather than straight ahead.

After mayflies emerge from the water as adults, you can sometimes see them resting on plants.

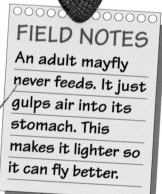

FIELD NOTES

An adult mayfly never feeds. It just gulps air into its stomach. This makes it lighter so it can fly better.

DRAGONFLY

The dragonfly is a fast and powerful flier. It has two pairs of long wings that it always holds stiffly away from its body. It has huge eyes and its eyesight is sharper than that of most insects.

WHERE TO FIND:
Dragonflies live around ponds and streams, but they can fly long distances, far from water.

WHAT TO LOOK FOR:

✶ SIZE
Dragonflies are between one and seven inches long.

✶ COLOR
Dragonflies are brightly colored. They vary from brown to red.

✶ OTHER FEATURES
They lay their eggs in water.

✶ BEHAVIOR
Some types of dragonfly simply fly in straight lines, back and forth over the patch of ground where they live.

Whether it is flying or resting, the dragonfly always has its wings outspread.

FIELD NOTES

With its spiny legs held forward, a dragonfly scoops up flies and other small insects in midair.

DAMSELFLY

Delicate damselflies are related to dragonflies, but they are smaller and do not fly as strongly. Instead of flying in a straight line like dragonflies do, damselflies flit around like butterflies.

FIELD NOTES

Damselflies rarely fly far from their pond or stream. Sometimes one may land on your shoulder.

Unlike dragonflies, damselflies close their wings when at rest.

WHAT TO LOOK FOR:

✳ SIZE
Damselflies are one to two inches long—about as long as your first finger.

✳ COLOR
They can be bright blue, green, violet, or even red.

✳ OTHER FEATURES
Damselfly larvae live in water.

✳ BEHAVIOR
Damselflies clean their eyes and antennae (an-TEN-ee) with their forelegs. They feed on gnats and midges.

BAND-WINGED GRASSHOPPER

Most grasshoppers are plain brown or green, but the band-winged grasshopper has bright red or yellow back wings, which it shows when it flies.

WHERE TO FIND:

In summer, you can often see band-winged grasshoppers on the ground in fields and by the roadside.

WHAT TO LOOK FOR:

✴ SIZE
The band-winged grasshopper is usually one to two inches long.

✴ COLOR
It looks grayish brown until it flies.

✴ OTHER FEATURES
The female buries its eggs in the ground in a case called an egg pod.

✴ BEHAVIOR
When it flies, it snaps its back wings. If disturbed, it uses its strong legs to jump away quickly.

You can tell if a band-winged grasshopper is young by its short wings.

FIELD NOTES

Male band-winged grasshoppers rub their wings over ridges on their hind legs to make their chirping call.

KATYDID

Katydids (KATE-ee-DIDZ) rest in trees during the day, but move around at night. To attract females, males rub their front wings together to make a call that sounds like *katydid*.

WHERE TO FIND:
On summer nights, katydids are drawn to bright lights. Look also in shrubs and in trees near forests.

WHAT TO LOOK FOR:

✳ SIZE
Katydids are one to two inches long.

✳ COLOR
They are often bright green and appear to be leaves until you look more closely.

✳ OTHER FEATURES
Katydids have long, whiplike antennae that stick out from their heads.

✳ BEHAVIOR
The female uses a long tube, called an ovipositor (oh-vuh-POZ-uht-uhr), to lay its eggs inside plants.

Katydids disguise themselves as leaves to hide from their predators.

FIELD NOTES

A katydid has no ears. In each front leg it has an organ called a tympanum (TIM-puh-num) which it hears through.

FIELD CRICKET

 Male field crickets make their well-known chirping call by rubbing their front wings together. Field crickets also have long, powerful back legs that they use for jumping.

WHERE TO FIND:
You can see field crickets on lawns and roadsides, in woods and fields, and sometimes inside houses.

WHAT TO LOOK FOR:

✳ SIZE
A field cricket is about one inch long.

✳ COLOR
It is black and shiny, with yellow marks on its forewings.

✳ OTHER FEATURES
It has wings that are folded flat over its back, but it does not fly well.

✳ BEHAVIOR
Adults live in burrows that they dig themselves. Some field crickets chirp more often during summer.

Field crickets have
large heads and
long antennae.

PRAYING MANTIS

 Praying mantises are long, narrow insects. They get their name from the way they hold their front legs folded together. This makes them look as if they are praying.

WHERE TO FIND:
Praying mantises often live in shrubs where they are hard to see because they are the same color as the leaves.

WHAT TO LOOK FOR:

✳ SIZE
Praying mantises can grow seven inches long—about as long as a pencil.

✳ COLOR
Most are green, but some are brown.

✳ OTHER FEATURES
A praying mantis has very powerful front legs, but its two pairs of hind legs are much thinner and weaker.

✳ BEHAVIOR
Praying mantises have wings, but they do not often fly.

Praying mantises sit on plants and wait for their prey to come near.

FIELD NOTES

To catch their prey, praying mantises kick out their spiny front legs and hook insects onto the spikes.

STICK INSECT

Stick insects are long and thin and have slender legs. They are sometimes called walking sticks. They stay still for long periods and move extremely slowly. Some people keep them as pets.

WHERE TO FIND:
Stick insects live in bushes, but they are difficult to spot because they look just like twigs.

WHAT TO LOOK FOR:

✳ **SIZE**
Stick insects range from two to ten inches long.

✳ **COLOR**
They are brown or green.

✳ **OTHER FEATURES**
Only a few kinds of stick insects have wings. Those without wings look most like sticks or twigs.

✳ **BEHAVIOR**
They feed mostly at night, on plants and leaves.

Stick insects often look like the plants they feed on. Predators find it hard to see them.

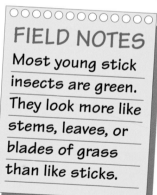

FIELD NOTES
Most young stick insects are green. They look more like stems, leaves, or blades of grass than like sticks.

TERMITE

 Termites live in colonies of many thousands. All have jobs. Soldier termites defend the group from enemies, workers gather food, and queen termites spend most of their time laying eggs.

WHERE TO FIND:
Termites eat wood and plants. They live in the ground, in old posts, or in buildings.

WHAT TO LOOK FOR:

✷ SIZE
Most termites are one-fifth to three-quarters of an inch long.

✷ COLOR
These insects are usually pale-colored.

✷ OTHER FEATURES
A queen carries thousands of eggs in her body, causing her body to swell. Queens can live for up to 15 years.

✷ BEHAVIOR
Soldier termites use their large jaws to attack enemies such as ants.

Worker termites, like this one, help look after the colony.

FIELD NOTES

Queen termites are so important that workers clean them and feed them mouth to mouth.

GIANT WATER BUG

 Giant water bugs feed on insects and other small creatures. They capture their prey with their strong front legs, then inject poison into the prey through their sharp beaks.

WHERE TO FIND:
Giant water bugs live in ponds. They are particularly easy to see because they are so large.

WHAT TO LOOK FOR:

＊ SIZE
The giant water bug is about one to two inches long.

＊ COLOR
They are a dark brownish color.

＊ OTHER FEATURES
Giant water bugs usually stay around water. They are often attracted by lights and fly toward them.

＊ BEHAVIOR
Females sometimes lay their eggs on the males' backs.

Male water bugs often carry eggs around on their backs until the eggs hatch.

A giant water bug is big enough to eat tiny fish. It uses its strong front legs to catch and hold the prey.

25

WATER STRIDER

Water striders are skinny bugs that balance on their long, thin legs and skate around on ponds and streams. They are often called pond skaters. Some kinds are found on the ocean.

FIELD NOTES

To move across water, a strider spreads its legs wide apart. This balances its weight so it won't sink.

WHERE TO FIND:

Water striders are very common. You can see them on the surfaces of ponds and slow-moving streams.

WHAT TO LOOK FOR:

✳ SIZE
A water strider is between a quarter- and a half-inch long.

✳ COLOR
Water striders are dark brown to blackish in color.

✳ OTHER FEATURES
Some kinds of water striders have wings and are able to fly.

✳ BEHAVIOR
Water striders eat small insects that fall into the water.

The water strider has long middle and back legs that are covered with hairs to help it float on the water.

ASSASSIN BUG

Assassin bugs grab other insects with their powerful front legs and inject them with poison from their beaks. Some species wait for their prey to come near, but others chase after it.

WHERE TO FIND:
Assassin bugs live on leaves, flowers, and trees, and sometimes in sand dunes.

WHAT TO LOOK FOR:

✳ **SIZE**
Assassin bugs are between a half inch and one inch long.

✳ **COLOR**
These bugs come in many colors, including brown and black.

✳ **OTHER FEATURES**
Some assassin bugs are oval-shaped, but others are long and thin.

✳ **BEHAVIOR**
Some assassin bugs can pass diseases on to people through their bite.

Most assassin bugs are brown, but some are much more colorful and blend with the plants on which they rest.

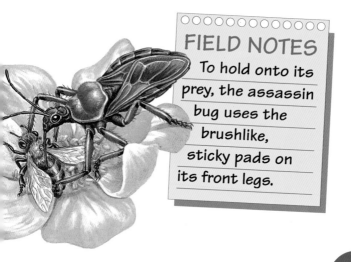

FIELD NOTES

To hold onto its prey, the assassin bug uses the brushlike, sticky pads on its front legs.

PERIODICAL CICADA

 Male cicadas (si-CADE-uhz) call loudly in summer, especially at the end of the day. They make the sound with organs, called tymbals (TIM-bals), in their abdomens.

WHERE TO FIND:
Cicadas are usually heard and not seen, but you may be lucky enough to spot one high up in a tree.

WHAT TO LOOK FOR:

* SIZE
Cicadas can be up to two inches long.

* COLOR
Most cicadas are dark-colored. They sometimes have green markings.

* OTHER FEATURES
They have bulging, reddish-colored eyes, flat bodies, and see-through wings.

* BEHAVIOR
Cicadas' mouthparts are shaped for piercing plants and sucking up juices. Each species has a different call.

Adult cicadas rest on tree trunks. Many are eaten by birds.

After hatching, a cicada nymph burrows into the soil. It lives there for as long as 17 years.

SPITTLEBUG

 Spittlebugs are tiny insects that get their name from the frothy bubbles their young leave behind on plants. The nymphs live inside these bubbles, which protect them as they grow into adults.

WHERE TO FIND:
Spittlebugs are too small to see easily, but you can look for their bubbles in summer on grass and weeds.

WHAT TO LOOK FOR:

✳ SIZE
Spittlebugs are one-eighth of an inch long.

✳ COLOR
Adults are usually brownish, but the nymphs are pale green.

✳ OTHER FEATURES
Adults have wings and can fly away from their enemies.

✳ BEHAVIOR
The plant juice the nymphs suck goes through their bodies, coming out as froth.

An adult spittlebug has a wide body and a large head.

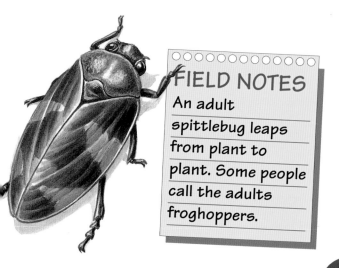

FIELD NOTES

An adult spittlebug leaps from plant to plant. Some people call the adults froghoppers.

ANT LION

These insects are called ant lions because the larvae capture and eat ants. Ant lion larvae live in the sand at the bottom of pits and wait for their prey to fall in. Then they grab the ants with their enormous jaws.

FIELD NOTES

Ant lion larvae throw sand at ants to make them fall over. It is then easy for the larvae to grab the ants.

An adult ant lion looks a little like a dragonfly.

WHERE TO FIND:

Ant lion larvae, sometimes called doodlebugs, live in dust and dry sand in woods and on plantations.

WHAT TO LOOK FOR:

✳ SIZE
Ant lion larvae are about three-quarters of an inch long. Adults are up to three inches long.

✳ COLOR
Adults and larvae are light brownish.

✳ OTHER FEATURES
Adults have long, thin bodies and wings. They are able to fly.

✳ BEHAVIOR
Adults are often attracted to bright lights at night.

GROUND BEETLE

 Many ground beetles are nocturnal. They rest during the day, but come out at night to find moth larvae and other prey. Although ground beetles can fly they prefer to stay on the ground.

WHERE TO FIND:
Ground beetles are common in woods and fields, where they rest under rocks and logs in the daytime.

WHAT TO LOOK FOR:

✳ SIZE
Ground beetles are between a quarter and a half inch long.

✳ COLOR
They are often shiny and black or metallic green.

✳ OTHER FEATURES
They usually have long, slender legs.

✳ BEHAVIOR
Some squirt out a liquid that gives off a nasty smell if you touch them. Many ground beetles are attracted to light.

Most ground beetles stay on the ground, but some climb trees in search of food.

One type of ground beetle frightens away its enemies by squirting a steamy, burning liquid into the air.

WHIRLIGIG BEETLE

 Large groups of whirligig beetles swirl around together on the water, paddling with their legs. They never bump into each other because they can sense the other beetles with their antennae. These oval-shaped insects feed on other small insects that fall into the water.

FIELD NOTES

Whirligig beetles have two pairs of eyes. One pair looks under the water. The other looks above it.

WHERE TO FIND:
Whirligigs live in pools and creeks. Adults usually stay on the surface, but the larvae live underwater.

WHAT TO LOOK FOR:

✳ SIZE
Whirligig beetles are about a half inch long.

✳ COLOR
These shiny beetles are usually black.

✳ OTHER FEATURES
If handled or attacked, some whirligig beetles release a milky liquid that smells like ripe apples.

✳ BEHAVIOR
Whirligigs can swim, dive below the surface, and even fly.

Whirligig beetles spin around quickly on the water's surface.

FIREFLY

Fireflies are sometimes called lightning bugs, because organs on the tips of their abdomens produce green or yellow flashing lights. Males and females flash the lights so they can find each other to mate.

WHERE TO FIND:
You can see firefly lights on summer nights in fields or near woods. During the day, fireflies often rest on plants.

WHAT TO LOOK FOR:

✳ SIZE
Fireflies are a quarter to three-quarters of an inch long.

✳ COLOR
They are brown or blackish, and often have yellow or orange stripes.

✳ OTHER FEATURES
Most female fireflies cannot fly.

✳ BEHAVIOR
Each species of firefly has its own recognizable light-flashing pattern. Fireflies eat small snails and slugs.

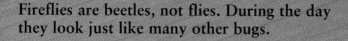

Fireflies are beetles, not flies. During the day they look just like many other bugs.

FIELD NOTES

Some fireflies attract other kinds of fireflies by copying their lights. Then they catch and eat the fireflies.

LADYBUG BEETLE

Many people welcome the brightly colored ladybug beetle—or ladybird—they find in their gardens. These beetles eat small pests such as aphids (AY-fids) and mites, which destroy plants and fruit trees.

WHERE TO FIND:
You are likely to see ladybugs right through summer on the leaves of many different plants.

WHAT TO LOOK FOR:

✳ **SIZE**
Ladybug beetles are about a quarter of an inch long.

✳ **COLOR**
Most are bright red with black spots. Others are orange or yellow.

✳ **OTHER FEATURES**
You most often see ladybugs crawling on plants, but they can also fly.

✳ **BEHAVIOR**
During the winter, ladybugs often cluster together under pieces of bark.

Ladybugs often gather in large swarms to hibernate during winter.

FIELD NOTES

A ladybug's bright color is a warning to its enemies that it tastes bad. Its nasty smell also protects it.

LONGHORN BEETLE

 The longhorn beetle gets its name from its antennae that are sometimes longer than its whole body. Through these antennae, the beetle picks up smells and vibrations from its surroundings.

WHERE TO FIND:

Look for adult longhorns around flowers. The larvae often live in the trunks and branches of trees.

WHAT TO LOOK FOR:

✳ SIZE
Longhorn beetles are a half inch to three inches long.

✳ COLOR
They can be brown, red, yellow, or green. Some are mottled or striped.

✳ OTHER FEATURES
Longhorns usually have oval eyes.

✳ BEHAVIOR
Longhorn beetle larvae often feed on wood, which means they are sometimes regarded as pests.

The adult longhorn beetle is easily recognized by its long, horn-shaped antennae.

FIELD NOTES

Some species scare away enemies by scraping their hind legs against their wings to make a loud creaking noise.

STAG BEETLE

 Male stag beetles have long, powerful jaws that look like the antlers of a stag. The beetles use these jaws when they fight fiercely against other stag beetles to defend their territory.

WHERE TO FIND:

You can see stag beetles around logs or on the ground in woods. The larvae live in rotting wood.

WHAT TO LOOK FOR:

✳ SIZE
Stag beetles are between one and two inches long.

✳ COLOR
They are black or reddish brown.

✳ OTHER FEATURES
They often fly around lights at night.

✳ BEHAVIOR
A female stag beetle's jaws are much smaller than a male's and not as strong. Adults eat leaves and tree bark. The larvae drink the juices of rotting wood.

Adult stag beetles are also known as pinching bugs because they sometimes pinch with their jaws.

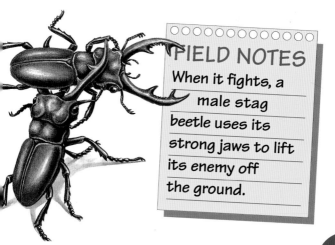

FIELD NOTES

When it fights, a male stag beetle uses its strong jaws to lift its enemy off the ground.

DUNG BEETLE

Dung beetles eat cattle dung and lay their eggs in it. They shape pieces of dung into balls and roll them away. Then they dig a tunnel and bury the dung balls under the ground to lay their eggs in.

WHERE TO FIND:

These beetles live wherever dung is found. The best place to see them is in cattle pastures.

WHAT TO LOOK FOR:

✳ SIZE
Dung beetles are one to two inches long.

✳ COLOR
They are different colors. Many are black or metallic green.

✳ OTHER FEATURES
Some have antennae shaped like horns.

✳ BEHAVIOR
They use their strong forelegs and claws to dig tunnels. Males and females often work in pairs to push huge balls of dung long distances to burial places.

Dung beetles are also known as tumblebugs because they tumble, or roll, balls of dung.

WEEVIL

Weevils are a kind of beetle. They eat plants, seeds, grains, and nuts. Most weevils have curved snouts with jaws at the end. A weevil uses its snout and jaws to drill into plants.

WHERE TO FIND:
Weevils eat cereals and grains and sometimes come into food cupboards. They are known as pests.

WHAT TO LOOK FOR:

* **SIZE**
Most weevils are only about an eighth of an inch long.

* **COLOR**
Most are dark brown to blackish.

* **OTHER FEATURES**
Some weevils have wings, but they rarely fly.

* **BEHAVIOR**
When weevils are disturbed, they sometimes stay so still that they seem to be dead.

Although most weevils are brown or black, some are brightly colored, like this one.

TIGER SWALLOWTAIL

 The back wings of a swallowtail butterfly end in two narrow "tails." A tiger swallowtail has bright black and yellow stripes, like those of a tiger.

WHERE TO FIND:

This butterfly is common in eastern North America. Look for it in fields and woods.

WHAT TO LOOK FOR:

✳ SIZE
Tiger swallowtails have wingspans from three and a half to four inches.

✳ COLOR
Most have black and yellow stripes, but some females are all black.

✳ OTHER FEATURES
Their larvae are dark green.

✳ BEHAVIOR
Swallowtails feed mainly on sugary nectar from flowers. Sometimes they eat mineral salts from muddy ground.

The tiger swallowtail is one of North America's largest swallowtail butterflies.

FIELD NOTES
The patterns on many butterflies' wings are made up of scales of a single color that overlap.

MONARCH BUTTERFLY

 Monarchs are the only butterflies that migrate. They fly south each fall and return north in spring when the weather is warmer. This is why they are also called "wanderers."

A monarch butterfly has large, colorful wings and small front legs.

FIELD NOTES

The milkweed the monarch caterpillar eats makes it taste bad. If a bird catches a monarch, it will spit it out.

Monarch butterflies live around flowers and milkweed plants, which are its main food.

WHAT TO LOOK FOR:

✳ SIZE
The monarch's wingspan is about four inches across.

✳ COLOR
Monarchs are brown or orange-brown, with black and white markings.

✳ OTHER FEATURES
Monarch caterpillars have black, yellow, and white stripes.

✳ BEHAVIOR
The caterpillars feed on poisonous milkweed plants.

SPHINX MOTH

 Sphinx (SFINX) moths have a long tube, called a proboscis (prah-BAHS-iss), that they use for sucking nectar from flowers. Sphinx moths are strong fliers and beat their wings rapidly.

WHERE TO FIND:

The best time to see sphinx moths is when they are feeding—usually around dusk or at night.

WHAT TO LOOK FOR:

✳ **SIZE**
A sphinx moth has a wingspan of two to four inches.

✳ **COLOR**
Sphinx moths come in many different colors. Many are reddish.

✳ **OTHER FEATURES**
The caterpillar has a curved spike at one end of its body to scare enemies.

✳ **BEHAVIOR**
The caterpillar feeds on plants such as tomatoes, and is considered a pest.

Sphinx moths are among the largest moths. They are also known as hawkmoths.

FIELD NOTES

Some sphinx moths have eyelike patterns on their wings to frighten away enemies.

LUNA MOTH

 Like a swallowtail butterfly, a luna moth has a long "tail" on each hind wing. A luna moth's wings also have markings that look like eyes. These help to frighten away birds and other enemies.

WHERE TO FIND:

Like most moths, luna moths fly about at night. Look for them around lights.

WHAT TO LOOK FOR:

✴ SIZE
The luna moth has a wingspan of up to three inches.

✴ COLOR
This moth is an unusual, delicate, pale-green color.

✴ OTHER FEATURES
Luna caterpillars are covered with spines that protect them from enemies.

✴ BEHAVIOR
The caterpillars feed on walnut and hickory leaves. Adults do not eat.

Luna moths are the largest moths in North America.

FIELD NOTES

Bats prey on all kinds of moths. Bats catch moths at night, while both are in flight.

CRANE FLY

Because they have such long, thin legs, crane flies are sometimes called daddy longlegs. Crane fly larvae are long, fat grubs called leatherjackets. They eat grass and sometimes ruin lawns.

FIELD NOTES

Some crane flies can live in very cold climates. They emerge early in spring and walk on the snow.

WHERE TO FIND:
Crane flies and their larvae live in gardens or around water. Summer is the best time to see them.

WHAT TO LOOK FOR:

✳ SIZE
Crane flies vary in length from one-third of an inch to one inch.

✳ COLOR
Crane flies are brownish or gray. Some have dark markings on their wings.

✳ OTHER FEATURES
Crane flies look like giant mosquitoes, but they do not bite.

✳ BEHAVIOR
They often fly low over the ground, with their legs hanging down loosely.

Crane flies often rest on garden plants.

MOSQUITO

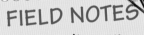 Mosquitoes (muh-SKEET-ohs) eat plant juices, but the females also bite animals and humans to suck their blood. They do this by piercing the skin with a sharp tube called a proboscis.

FIELD NOTES

A mosquito can flap its wings 600 times in the seconds it takes you to say "mosquito" slowly!

WHAT TO LOOK FOR:

❋ **SIZE**
Mosquitoes are about a quarter of an inch long.

❋ **COLOR**
Mosquitoes are brownish.

❋ **OTHER FEATURES**
They lay their eggs on water. The larvae live under the water's surface until they can fly away.

❋ **BEHAVIOR**
Female mosquitoes suck blood because this helps their eggs to develop.

Mosquitoes have thin bodies and long, thin legs.

ROBBER FLY

Robber flies eat other insects that they often catch while flying. Once it catches an insect, the robber fly holds the prey in its long legs and sucks its juices with its sharp mouthparts. Most robber flies are large and hairy, but others are thin with skinny legs.

FIELD NOTES

Robber flies catch bees and other stinging prey, as well as insects bigger than themselves.

Robber flies often sit on twigs as they watch for prey.

WHERE TO FIND:
Look for robber flies on tree trunks or on the tips of twigs. These insects are common and widespread.

WHAT TO LOOK FOR:

✳ SIZE
Robber flies are a half inch to one and a half inches long.

✳ COLOR
These insects are brownish-yellow.

✳ OTHER FEATURES
A robber fly has tough bristles around its mouth that protect it from injury as it holds onto struggling prey.

✳ BEHAVIOR
Some robber flies look like stinging bees or wasps. This scares off enemies.

HOVER FLY

 Hover flies get their name because they seem to float, or hover, in the air around plants. Like bees, hover flies play an important part in spreading pollen from plant to plant.

WHERE TO FIND:
Look for adult hover flies around flowers and bushes in fields, parks, and gardens.

WHAT TO LOOK FOR:

✳ SIZE
Hover flies are usually between a quarter- and a half-inch long.

✳ COLOR
Hover flies often have yellow and black bands on their bodies.

✳ OTHER FEATURES
They have very large eyes for a small insect—and good eyesight.

✳ BEHAVIOR
The larvae help to protect plants because they feed on pests called aphids.

Adult hover flies feed on the nectar from flowers.

Wasp   Hover fly

YELLOW JACKET

Yellow jackets are wasps that have brightly colored, striped bodies. The adults feed on fruit and nectar from flowers. The larvae eat insects that worker wasps find and bring to them.

WHERE TO FIND:
Yellow jackets fly around flowers in summer. They are sometimes attracted to picnic food.

WHAT TO LOOK FOR:

✳ SIZE
Yellow jackets are a half to three-quarters of an inch long.

✳ COLOR
They have black and yellow bands.

✳ OTHER FEATURES
Some yellow jackets build nests in the ground. Others make their nests in safe places aboveground.

✳ BEHAVIOR
Female yellow jackets will sting anything that disturbs their nests.

When they are not in flight, yellow jackets hold their wings close to their bodies.

FIELD NOTES
Yellow jackets build paperlike nests with special compartments to hold their eggs and larvae.

HONEYBEE

Bees carry pollen from flower to flower, helping plants to reproduce. They also make honey from flower nectar. Honeybees live in hives, where the honey is stored and where the larvae live.

WHERE TO FIND:
Honeybees are most often seen around flowers. You might spot a hive in a hollow tree.

WHAT TO LOOK FOR:

✳ SIZE
Honeybees are about a half inch long.

✳ COLOR
Honeybees have orange and black stripes and many yellowish hairs.

✳ OTHER FEATURES
Honeybees have poisonous stingers that they jab at enemies.

✳ BEHAVIOR
Bees live in colonies with a queen that lays the eggs and thousands of female worker bees. There are only a few males.

Female worker bees, like this honeybee, gather most of the pollen and nectar for the hive.

○○○○○○○○○○○○○○○

FIELD NOTES

All bees do special dances to show each other how far away flowers are—and in which direction.

BUMBLEBEE

Bumblebees get their name from the humming or "bumbling" sound they make as they fly. They nest in the ground, often in deserted mouse nests. These bees live in large colonies with a queen, up to 80,000 female workers, and males called drones.

FIELD NOTES

Skunks often dig up bumblebee nests. Then they eat the bees as well as the honey the bees make.

A bumblebee's body is round and hairy.

WHERE TO FIND:
Bumblebees are common.
You can see them buzzing
around flowers, from
which they collect pollen.

WHAT TO LOOK FOR:

✳ SIZE
Bumblebees are a little bigger than
honeybees—up to one inch long.

✳ COLOR
They have yellow and black markings.

✳ OTHER FEATURES
They have stiff hairs on their legs.
These hairs brush against the inside of
flowers, where pollen sticks to them.

✳ BEHAVIOR
These bees defend themselves against
attackers by stinging them.

ANT

 Ants live in large colonies that are ruled by one egg-laying female, called the queen. When they are looking for food, ants leave a trail of scent on the ground for others in the colony to follow.

WHERE TO FIND:
Although most ants nest underground, you may see them searching for food such as plants and insects.

WHAT TO LOOK FOR:

✳ SIZE
Ants are one-eighth to three-quarters of an inch long.

✳ COLOR
They vary from red to brown or black.

✳ OTHER FEATURES
Queens are wingless because they bite off their own wings after mating.

✳ BEHAVIOR
Ants work in teams to find food, to look after their young, and to defend themselves against enemies.

Leafcutter ants, found in Louisiana and Texas, cut out pieces of leaf to help make their food.

FIELD NOTES

Some kinds of ants capture the young of other ants and make them work as slaves.

GLOSSARY

Abdomen An insect's body is divided into three parts—the head; the middle section, called the thorax, where the wings and legs are attached; and the tail section, called the abdomen.

Antennae Feelers on an insect's head that are used to pick up smells and vibrations from the air.

Colony A group of insects that live together.

Drone A male honeybee.

Dung Animal droppings.

Dusk The time just before nightfall when it is almost dark.

Hibernate When an insect sleeps through winter so it does not need to eat.

Larva An insect's wormlike stage between the egg and adult stages. Moth and butterfly larvae are called caterpillars.

Mate An adult insect's male or female partner with which it produces young.

Migrate To move from one place to another.

Nectar The sugary liquid that flowers produce.

Nocturnal To sleep or rest during the day and eat and move around only at night.

Nymph The young, wingless stage of some insects between the egg and adult stages.

Organ A part of the body, such as the heart or brain, that helps the body to function.

Pollen The fine, yellow powder made by flowers so they can reproduce.

Predator Any creature that hunts other creatures for food.

Prey Any creature that is hunted by other creatures for food.

Scent A smell. Animals often have their own scent that helps them recognize each other.

Territory The place where an animal lives, in which it feels safe, and that it defends.

Tymbal A part of an insect's body that vibrates to make a noise.

Vibration A very quick, small movement back and forth.

Wingspan The distance from wingtip to wingtip when the wings are outstretched.

INDEX OF
INSECTS

PHOTOGRAPHIC CREDITS

The world's largest nonprofit scientific and educational organization, the National Geographic Society was founded in 1888 "for the increase and diffusion of geographic knowledge." Since then it has supported scientific exploration and spread information to its more than eight million members worldwide.

The National Geographic Society educates and inspires millions every day through magazines, books, television programs, videos, maps and atlases, research grants, the National Geographic Bee, teacher workshops, and innovative classroom materials.

The Society is supported through membership dues, charitable gifts, and income from the sale of its educational products.

Members receive NATIONAL GEOGRAPHIC magazine—the Society's official journal—discounts on Society products, and other benefits.

For more information about the National Geographic Society, its educational programs, publications, or ways to support its work, please call 1-800-NGS-LINE (647-5463), or write to the following address:

National Geographic Society
1145 17th Street, N.W.
Washington, D.C. 20036-4688 U.S.A.

Visit the Society's Web site: www.nationalgeographic.com